THE ATTACK ON PEARL HARBOR

The Attack that Shook America

Written by Victoria Domingos Valentim
In collaboration with Mathieu Roger
Translated by Rebecca Neal

History 50MINUTES.com

THE ATTACK ON PEARL HARBOR

KEY INFORMATION

- **When:** 7 December 1941.
- **Where:** Pearl Harbor (US air and naval base on the island of Oahu, Hawaii, in the Pacific Ocean).
- **Context:** the Second World War (1939-1945).
- **Countries involved:** the United States against the Empire of Japan.
- **Key protagonists:**
  - Walter Campbell Short, American general (1880-1949).
  - Husband Edward Kimmel, American admiral (1882-1968).
  - Isoroku Yamamoto, Japanese admiral (1884-1943).
  - Mitsuo Fuchida, Japanese commander (1902-1976).
- **Outcome:** Japanese victory.
- **Victims:**
  - American side: 2403 dead or missing and 1178 wounded.
  - Japanese side: 64 dead and one prisoner.

INTRODUCTION

The surprise attack on Pearl Harbor by Japan on 7 December 1941 is one of the most famous incidents of the Second World War. Led by the admiral Isoroku Yamamoto, the offensive on the American air and naval base situated on one of the Hawaiian Islands caused the USA to join the war on the side of the Allies. By endangering the American fleet, the Japanese wanted to neutralise the great power in order to establish the Greater East Asia Co-Prosperity Sphere and, in this way, push the Western powers out of the Pacific. This attack therefore was clearly a part of Japan's imperial expansion policy.

Carried out in two successive aerial waves, the raid inflicted substantial human and material loss in the space of two hours. On the American side, 2403 men were killed and 1178 were wounded. There was also serious material damage: four battleships were sunk and a further four were damaged; 13 ships were sunk or damaged; and 188 planes were destroyed and 159 were seriously damaged. The Japanese losses were more limited: 64 men died, one sailor was captured, and 29 planes and five submarines were destroyed. However, although the attack on Pearl Harbor – which even today remains controversial – seems, at first glance, to have been a complete success for the Japanese, it was in fact a failure because they left the repair shops and fuel depots intact, allowing the United States to recover.

SOCIAL AND POLITICAL CONTEXT

THE BEGINNINGS OF THE SECOND WORLD WAR

The Second World War is one of the best-known and deadliest conflicts in history. It pitted two camps against each other: the Allies and the Axis.

GOOD TO KNOW

The Axis, also known as the Rome-Berlin-Tokyo Axis, was an alliance formed in September 1940, when Germany, Italy and Japan signed the Tripartite Pact. This agreement aimed to create a new order in Europe through the intervention of Germany and Italy, and in the Far East thanks to Japan. In addition to these three countries, Hungary and Bulgaria also took part in the alliance. However, the Axis powers never came together to carry out joint operations.

The Allies were all the countries that were opposed to the Axis powers during the Second World War. They included the United Kingdom, France, Belgium, Luxembourg, Poland, the United States and the Republic of China.

In the wake of the First World War (1914-1918), the victorious countries signed the Treaty of Versailles (1919), which aimed to re-establish peace and define the sanctions to be imposed on Germany, judged to be responsible for the conflict. Germany's territory was then reorganised and over 10% of its land was shared among various countries. Measures were also taken to weaken its army by seizing many planes, cannons, etc., and by abolishing compulsory military service. The country's economy was also badly affected because Germany was forced to pay reparations for the damage suffered by France and Belgium.

Photograph taken during the signing of the Treaty of Versailles.

These sanctions very quickly led to dissatisfaction from the heads of state opposed to the Allies during the conflict. Germany was determined to act: it adopted protectionist measures and embarked on an expansionist policy based on the principle of living space, in this way conquering land judged necessary for the survival of the German people. Its neighbour Poland was the first victim: on 1 September 1939, it was invaded by Germany. This event triggered the Second War, which played out in three theatres of operations:

- Europe (Poland, the United Kingdom, Finland, Denmark, Norway, France, Belgium, the Netherlands, Luxembourg, Greece, Italy, Germany and the USSR);
- Africa and the Middle East (North Africa, Iraq, Syria, Lebanon and Iran);
- Asia (China, Japan, Southeast Asia, Indochina, the Pacific Islands, and islands close to Japan such as Iwo Jima and Okinawa).

JAPANESE EXPANSIONISM

Starting in the 19th century, during the Meiji period (1868-1912, from the name of the Emperor Meiji), the Empire of Japan embarked on a phase of territorial, economic, political and military expansion in East Asia. In this context, the island of Formosa (Taiwan, 1895), the south of the island of Sakhalin (mountainous Russian island, 1905) and Korea (1910) were annexed.

During the First World War, Japan seized German territory in the Far East, to the detriment of the Europeans and Americans, who were also present in the region. However, from the 1920s onwards, Japanese economic growth slowed down due to a lack of raw materials and employment prospects. Ten years later, the economic crisis propelled the Japanese nationalists and military to power. The Empire of the Rising Sun continued its conquests: in 1931, the Imperial Japanese Army invaded Manchuria, before invading the rest of China in 1937, driven by a desire to set up a Greater East Asia Co-Prosperity Sphere in order to make the Asian states self-sufficient and distance them from all Western intervention.

Faced with this territorial expansion which threatened American interests, the United States intervened and signed the Washington Naval Treaty (1922), which sought to reduce the naval fleets of the signatories (the United Kingdom, France, Italy, the United States and Japan). A few years later, the pact was modified by the London Naval Treaty (1930), which further limited naval shipbuilding. However, Tokyo judged these restrictions to be excessive and decided to stop adhering to them.

In spite of the palpable tension between the United States and Japan between 1935 and 1937 – when Japan sunk the American warship *USS Panay*, which was at that point in the Republic of China – the Americans did not react and chose not to intervene in what would become the beginnings of a new global conflict. Laws on neutrality were passed in order to stop them from taking a stance on foreign conflicts, in this way drawing a lesson from a number of losses sustained during the First World War. However, in the Quarantine Speech he delivered in 1937, the president of the United States Franklin D. Roosevelt (1882-1945) declared his opposition to dictatorial systems and condemned the Japanese dictatorship.

The situation between the two countries only worsened from then on, and 26 July 1941 marked the peak of the discord between the two powers. A few days previously, an Imperial Conference had been held in Japan, bringing together the emperor, members of the government and military leaders in order to establish the Greater East Asia Co-Prosperity Sphere. In particular, it had been decided that if this space was not recognised by the United States, the Japanese would not hesitate to respond with force. Furthermore, all the merchant ships still present in the Atlantic were ordered to return to Japan. From then on, the United States, the Netherlands and the United Kingdom decreed a complete embargo on oil and steel, as well as the freezing of Japanese assets on American soil. In response, the Japanese decided to declare war on the United States and the United Kingdom on the 6 September 1941. By the end of November, negotiations between the USA and Japan had come to nothing: while the Japanese demanded that the Americans put an end to the support they were giving to China, the American Secretary of State Cordell Hull (1871-1955) demanded the withdrawal of Japanese troops from the country. The situation quickly became critical and the Japanese decided to take action.

On 3 November, the admiral Osami Nagano (1880-1947) gave details of the plan to attack Pearl Harbor prepared by Isoroku Yamamoto, which was approved by Emperor Hirohito (1901-1989) a few days later. Following fruitless negotiations, the Imperial General Headquarters of Japan implemented the plan to attack the American fleet and ordered the Admiral Yamamoto to begin the mission against Pearl Harbor.

THE UNITED STATES AND THE SECOND WORLD WAR

During the Second World War, the Americans actively helped Great Britain, the Soviet Union, China and Free France. Initially, the USA's involvement in the conflict was limited. It mainly provided war material (planes, tanks, weapons, etc.), food and financial support. In this way, over 50 billion dollars' worth of supplies were lent to the Allied forces between 1941 and 1945, in accordance with the Lend-Lease policy approved on 11 March 1941.

While they were expecting a reaction from Germany for the aid provided to the Allies, on 7 December 1941, the United States were attacked by Japan, thousands of miles from the theatre of operations. From that day onwards, the USA had officially entered the war on the side of the Allies.

KEY PROTAGONISTS

HUSBAND EDWARD KIMMEL, AMERICAN ADMIRAL

Born in 1882, Husband Edward Kimmel was the Commander-in-Chief of the American fleet in the Pacific when Pearl Harbor was attacked in 1941. After the offensive, he was accused of negligence and held responsible for the loss of the naval base. He was criticised for not taking the information and warnings that preceded the attack seriously. Afterwards, he was demoted to the role of rear admiral (the equivalent of brigadier general) while he planned reprisals to be carried out against Japan. Overwhelmed by accusations, he took early retirement in 1942 and never stopped defending himself thereafter. In 1955, he published a book, *Admiral Kimmel's Story*, in which he described the attack on Pearl Harbor and refuted the criticism he had received. He died on 14 May 1968 in Connecticut.

WALTER CAMPBELL SHORT, AMERICAN GENERAL

Portrait of General Walter Campbell Short.

Walter Campbell Short was born in 1880 and joined the American army in March 1902. His rise was swift and successful. In 1941, he was made lieutenant general in the United States Army and appointed to the Hawaiian command, which made him responsible for the defence of Pearl Harbor. During his assignment, he was convinced that the most immediate danger facing the American fleet was sabotage, so he decided to gather all the planes together and put them in locations where they were easy to monitor. Unfortunately, this decision was to have serious consequences, as it made it easier for the Japanese to destroy the American planes. In addition, Short underestimated the effectiveness of radar and only provided for a surveillance team between 4am and 7am.

In view of all these mistakes, Short appeared to be an obvious target for blame for the American army in the immediate aftermath of the attack. In 1942, he was stripped of his command and demoted to the rank of major general, which hastened his departure from the army on 28 February 1942. He died on 9 March 1949, at the age of 68. Several years later, the American Senate passed a resolution exonerating Short and restoring him to the rank of admiral.

ISOROKU YAMAMOTO, JAPANESE ADMIRAL

Photograph of Admiral Yamamoto, taken in 1940.

Isoroku Yamamoto was born in 1884, and was one of the most emblematic Japanese figures of the Second World War. In mid-August 1939, he was named Commander-in-

Chief of the Japanese Combined Fleet. Contrary to popular belief, it would seem that Yamamoto was in favour of the war. Once he had received Emperor Hirohito's order to attack the Americans, he made the attack on Pearl Harbor his main objective. After the offensive, he took part in the Battle of Midway (5-7 June 1942), which ended in defeat for the Japanese. Yamamoto died in 1943 during an aerial reconnaissance mission.

The Battle of Midway (an island situated around 1200 miles from the Hawaiian Islands) pitted Japan against the United States. The American intelligence services, which had successfully deciphered threatening enemy messages, alerted the American admiral Chester William Nimitz (1885-1966), who gave the order on 27 and 30 May for three aircraft carriers to be sent to the island. After a weak response, 50 bombers managed to sink the four Japanese aircraft carriers, securing victory for the Americans.

MITSUO FUCHIDA, JAPANESE COMMANDER

Mitsuo Fuchida was born in 1902 and entered the Imperial Japanese Naval Academy in 1921. He was soon promoted to the rank of lieutenant commander and accepted into the Naval Staff College. In 1939, he became commander of the air group of the aircraft carrier *Akagi*, which was used during the attack on Pearl Harbor, and coordinated preparations for the offensive. On 7 December 1941, he led the first attack wave.

On 19 February 1942, he led the Bombing of Darwin (Northern Australia). After the war, Fuchida converted to Christianity after listening to several testimonies from prisoners of war who spoke of God and faith. He died in 1976.

GOOD TO KNOW

The Bombing of Darwin took place on 19 February 1942, and its similarities with the attack on Pearl Harbor have often caused the two of them to be compared. This raid was the first attack on Australia, which until that point had sustained little damage during the Second World War. The two waves of attacks were a success for the Japanese in material terms, but also in psychological terms, as the inhabitants were left very shaken.

ANALYSIS OF THE ATTACK

The Pearl Harbor naval base had been built between 1906 and 1908 and was situated in the Hawaiian Islands, which were on the way to the Philippines, an American protectorate, and to the Dutch Indies, Malaysia and Oceania. This base therefore occupied a very important strategic position and housed six to eight battleships and three aircraft carriers, as well as cruisers, destroyers, submarines, minelayers and auxiliary vessels.

Aerial view of the Pearl Harbor military base shortly before the Japanese attack.

There were also fuel depots, dry docks and repair workshops to maintain the fleet. In total, over 25 000 men were present on the base. In order to prevent any attacks, a large number of planes were also stored there. Thanks to all this, Pearl Harbor seemed impregnable. In any case, this is what Walter Campbell Short, commander of the land forces on the island, claimed prior to the attack: "Here in Hawaii we all live in a citadel or gigantically fortified island" (Prange, 1991: 97).

THE PREPARATIONS

The attack on Pearl Harbour was devised at the start of 1941 by the admiral Isoroku Yamamoto. In order to establish a plan of attack, he drew inspiration in particular from the raid carried out by the admiral Tōgō Heihachirō (1848-1934) against the Russian fleet at Port Arthur (former name of the Chinese city of Lüshun, North-East China) in 1904.

Arthur in 1897. However, Japan opposed its domination of Manchuria (North-East China) and planned to recover this section of territory, leading to the outbreak of the Russo-Japanese War. On 7 August 1904, the Japanese launched an assault on Port Arthur by sending several waves of suicide missions (kamikazes).

Detailed preparation for the attack on a model.

At the end of August, Yamamoto revealed his plan of attack to several general officers, including the admiral Osami Nagano. The project was then studied at the Naval School, which raised a number of objections concerning in particular the unfavourable weather conditions. Indeed, the attack was planned for December, and heavy storms were forecast for that time of year. Furthermore, some experts suggested that it would be more prudent to launch the offensive closer to the coasts of Japan. However, in spite of these warnings, Yamamoto remained convinced of the need to wipe out the American fleet in Pearl Harbor, for two reasons:

- firstly, the majority of the American fleet in the South Pacific was stationed there;
- secondly, Yamamoto judged that the American fleet was the greatest obstacle to the Japanese in their expansionist initiative.

His plan of attack was finally officially approved on 3 November 1941 by the admiral Chūichi Nagumo (1887-1944). On 7 November, Nagumo was named commander of the attack fleet for Pearl Harbor and, on 2 December, the Imperial Council decided to declare war on the United States.

THE OBJECTIVES AND STRATEGY OF THE ATTACK

The aim of Yamamoto's plan was both defensive and offensive. Firstly, it aimed to ensure an adequate oil supply for the war against China, which the presence of the United States did not allow in the state of affairs at that time. Secondly, it sought to weaken the United States and force them to accept Japan's conquests and the establishment of the Greater East Asia Co-Prosperity Sphere.

The Greater East Asia Co-Prosperity Sphere was suggested in 1936 by the Japanese Minister for Foreign Affairs, Hachirō Arita (1875-1965), and unveiled on 4 August 1940 by his successor, Yōsuke Matsuoka (1880-1946). The idea was to create a self-sufficient bloc of Asian countries led by Japan, whose primary goal was colonial expansion to the detriment of the Western occupiers. The Co-Prosperity Sphere extended towards near Australia to the sSouth, Singapore to the west and Guam, Wake and Midway to the east.

In order to successfully execute his plan, Yamamoto planned to take the American naval base by surprise. To do this, he decided to launch the offensive on a Sunday, when the fleet would be at Pearl Harbor for the weekend and not all of the crews would be present. Furthermore, the attack was planned for the morning so as to avoid the challenges of night navigation and bombardments.

On 6 December 1941, the Japanese Minister for Foreign Affairs tasked the ambassador Kichisaburō Nomura (1877-1964) with delivering a coded message to the American Secretary of State which should reach Washington on 7 December at 1pm (7:30am in Hawaii). The message contained a declaration of war, but the American authorities were unable to decode it all. Nonetheless, General George Catlett Marshall (1880-1959), worried by the content of the mysterious message, decided to alert the American bases in the Philippines, Panama, San Diego and Pearl Harbor. However, due to technical failures, the message arrived too late and the bombing had already begun.

THE ATTACK

The Japanese had gathered considerable resources to destroy the American fleet: two battleships, two heavy cruisers, 11 light cruisers, 11 destroyers, three submarines, eight supply vessels and six aircraft carriers.

Furthermore, two types of attack were planned to maximise the chances of success: a surprise attack and an attack if they lost the element of surprise. In the first case, the offensive would unfold in successive phases: torpedo bombers (bombers used to attack ships or submarines) would attack first, followed by bombers, with fighter planes ensuring their protection. If the element of surprise was lost, all the Japanese forces would attack at the same time; in that case, aerodromes, equipment and torpedo bombers would be attacked. In order to tell the pilots which tactic to adopt, it had been agreed that one flare would be sent up for the surprise attack and two for the second option. However, when the time came to launch the offensive and Fuchida opted for the surprise attack, he noticed that some pilots had not seen his first signal and thus sent up a second flare. Consequently, some pilots thought he had opted for the second kind of attack, and the entire Japanese fleet simultaneously attacked the American fleet.

The first wave

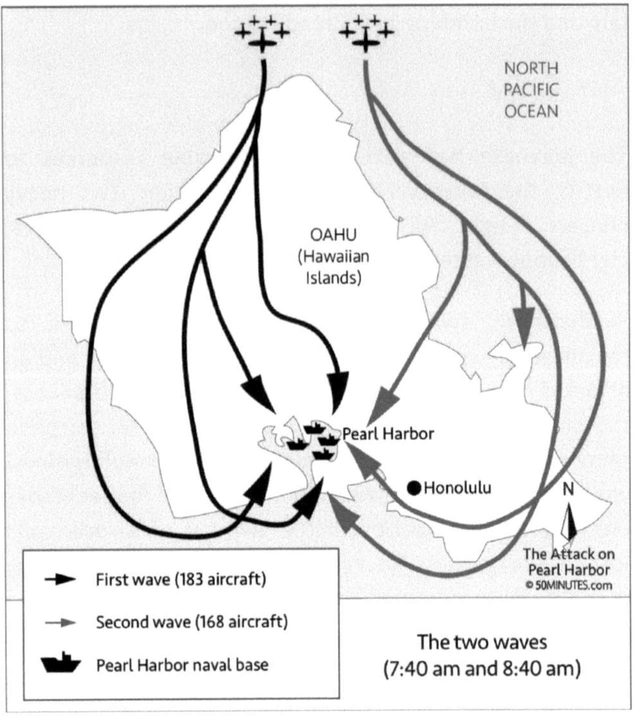

At 3:42am, a first submarine was sent to carry out reconnaissance at Pearl Harbor. The American minesweeper *USS
Condor* noticed it and warned the American destroyer *USS
Ward* a few minutes later. *USS Ward* set out to look for
the Japanese submarine, but could not find it. At 6:37am,
another Japanese submarine was sighted by *USS Ward* and
destroyed.

Half an hour later, the first attack wave, led by Captain Mitsuo Fuchida and made up of 183 aeroplanes (49 bombers, 40 torpedo bombers, 51 dive bombers and 43 fighter jets) set off.

At 7:02am, two American soldiers were monitoring the radar station in the North of Oahu when they noticed some planes. They warned the lieutenant Kermit Arthur Tyler (1913-2010), but Tyler was convinced that they were the B-17 planes they were expecting and decided not to raise the alarm. At 7:58am, with the American soldiers not expecting to be attacked, the first Japanese bombs were dropped. Convinced that the surprise attack had succeeded, five minutes after giving the order to attack, Fushida gave the signal "Tora... Tora... Tora..." ("Tiger... Tiger... Tiger") to the aircraft carriers. This was the code that had previously been agreed upon and was intended for Chūichi Nagumo as an indication that the surprise attack had been a success. The American soldiers were caught unawares and still did not know who was attacking them. Nonetheless, Don Stratton (born in 1922), a sailor on the *USS Arizona*, later explained that when the Americans saw the red sun on the planes' fuselage, they knew that it was the Japanese (*Seconds From Disaster: Pearl Harbor*, 2011).

At 8:02am, the American response began, but the soldiers were soon running low on ammunition. Furthermore, the Japanese planes were flying too high for the American weaponry to reach them. At 8:10am, the *USS Arizona*, which has now become a symbol of the attack, was attacked by ten Japanese bombers. Helped by the 450 tonnes of ammunition on board, a chain of explosions completely destroyed the ship and killed most of the men on board.

At the same time, the Hickam Air Force Base, to the South of Pearl Harbor, was attacked by Japanese bombers. At 8:30am, the first attack wave stopped. The Americans made the most of the lull to take to the air with several fighter planes and to prepare for a second attack.

The second wave

One hour later, the second wave of planes, led by the lieutenant commander Shigekazu Shimazaki (1908-1945), took off. It comprised 54 high-altitude bombers, 78 bombers and 36 fighter jets, a total of 168 planes flying towards Pearl Harbor. This second attack ended at 9:45am.

Japanese planes ready for takeoff to attack Pearl Harbor.

When the attack on Pearl Harbor began, the men on board the ships were still sleeping. It was only at 7:58am, at the start of the bombardments, that the commander Logan Ramsey (1921-2000) raised the alarm. While the American soldiers tried to respond, the air force was sent on a search mission to the North and South of Pearl Harbor. Even though the situation was disastrous, the American soldiers did not give in and some even demonstrated great heroism. Those who stood out in the defence of the fleet include Doris Miller (1919-1943), a cook on board the *USS West Virginia*, who defended his ship by firing on the Japanese planes with an anti-aircraft machine gun. For this act of bravery, he was decorated with the Navy Cross in 1942.

A relative victory

The human toll of the attack on Pearl Harbor was overwhelming. On the American side, 2403 men died and 1178 were wounded. The material losses were no less catastrophic: in total, around 188 planes were destroyed and 159 were damaged. However, after the attack the base at Pearl Harbor remained operational and 80% of the ships were repaired.

On the Japanese side, the human and material losses were limited: 64 soldiers died and one was taken prisoner, 29 planes were shot down, and five submarines were sunk.

Although the attack on Pearl Harbor appeared to the Japanese to be a complete victory, in reality it proved to be a failure. Thanks to the discovery of military archives that had for a long time remained secret, researchers have been able to highlight the strategic mistakes of the attackers. The historian Tosh Minohara, who took part in the research, has identified four Japanese blunders:

- The first error is that they withdrew too soon. At 3pm, convinced that the American fleet had been wiped out, Chūichi Nagumo ordered his troops to withdraw and looked set to return to Japan as a hero. In doing so, he wanted to avoid the destruction of his fleet in a second raid and limit the number of men lost.
- Secondly, the assault was launched when the American aircraft carriers were not at Pearl Harbor. This can be explained by the fact that the Japanese did not know the real position of the American aircraft carriers when they were preparing for the attack. They only learnt that the carriers were not in the port six hours before the raid: two had been requisitioned to transport planes, and the third was being repaired. While Yamamoto thought that they should cancel the offensive, as he considered the

aircraft carriers to be its main target, Nagumo thought that attacking the battleships would be enough and took the decision to attack Pearl Harbor.

- Thirdly, the Japanese failed to attack points that were not protected by the Americans, such as the shipyard, the submarines and the fuel storage facility. The decision not to attack the fuel depots was taken by Yamamoto when the plan was first drawn up, as the admiral thought that bombing these oil reserves would produce vast amounts of smoke, reducing visibility for the Japanese aviators.

- The fourth mistake was attacking Pearl Harbor with no real declaration of war. Although the coded message had been sent, it had been received too late and could not be decoded and retranscribed in time. When the American intelligence services intercepted the message from Tokyo, they suspected that an operation was being prepared, but the decoding and retranscription took too long. When the different bases in the Pacific were finally warned, it was too late: the attack on Pearl Harbor had already begun.

IMPACT OF THE ATTACK

ON THE WAY TO A GLOBAL CONFLICT

The attack on Pearl Harbor was the event which triggered the USA's entry into the Second World War on the side of the Allies. The day after the attack, the president of the United States, Franklin D. Roosevelt, said: "Yesterday, December 7, 1941—a date which will live in infamy—the United States of America was suddenly and deliberately attacked by naval and air forces of the Empire of Japan. [...] I ask that the Congress declare that since the unprovoked and dastardly attack by Japan on Sunday, December 7th, 1941, a state of war has existed between the United States and the Japanese empire." (cited in Chan, 2016).

On 22 December 1941, during the Arcadia Conference in Washington, Winston Churchill (British statesman, 1874-1965) and Franklin D. Roosevelt joined forces against Nazi Germany. There followed a number of other important decisions:

- On 1 January 1942, the Declaration by United Nations was signed by the United States, Great Britain, China and the Soviet Union. In this document, the signatories agreed to participate in the war, to not give in until victory and to not sign a separate peace in order to defend liberty, human rights and justice.
- On 6 January 1942, the USA transformed its economy in order to respond to the needs of war, in particular with the announcement of the Victory Program, which

the president entrusted to the Secretary of War, Henry Lewis Stimson (1867-1950). Stimson planned to put the American economy at the service of the Allies, in particular by producing large quantities of war material and mobilising vast human resources.

With the entry of the United States into the war, the conflict was now global.

THE REACTIONS OF THE AXIS AND JAPAN

Following the attack on Pearl Harbor, Adolf Hitler (1889-1945) considered the United States' entry into the war inevitable. On 11 December 1941, four days after the Japanese offensive, Italy and Nazi Germany, Japan's allies, declared war on the superpower and attacked various British and

American colonies and military bases in Asia and the Pacific.

For its part, Japan considered the reaction of the United States to be too strong, as it viewed the attack on Pearl Harbor as legitimate and a consequence of multiple attacks and threats from America. This feeling of legitimacy remained in the minds of the Japanese for a long time: in 1991, the Japanese Minister for Foreign Affairs pointed out that Japan had sent a message to the United States 25 minutes before the start of the attack on Pearl Harbor.

CONTROVERSY: WAS ROOSEVELT GUILTY?

The attack on Pearl Harbor has been a controversial subject among the general public and military and state authorities. Immediately after the raid, inquiries were opened to look into the responsibility and negligence of various figures. As such, between December 1941 and July 1946, seven administrative commissions and one special commission were set up. The first inquiry (1942) was headed by Owen Roberts (US Supreme Court Associate Justice, 1875-1955) and accused Walter Campbell Short and Husband Edward Kimmel of dereliction of duty in their defence of the naval base.

They were not the only ones to be accused of negligence. Indeed, the role played by President Franklin D. Roosevelt during the attack on Pearl Harbor has frequently been called into question. Some believe that he was complicit and duplicitous. This 'revisionist' interpretation was primarily spread by enemies of the president and by opponents of his foreign policy at the time. These included the rear admiral Robert Albert Theobald (1884-1957), who evoked "President

Roosevelt's strategy of coring Japan to war by unremitting and ever-increasing diplomatic-economic pressure, and by simultaneously holding our fleet in Hawaii as an invitation to a surprise attack" (Theobald, 2006: 39). The American historian John Toland (1912-2004), in a book published in 1982, also supported the theory that the series of mistakes committed on the day of the attack on Pearl Harbor is too incredible not to be a sign of a plot. However, while all revisionists agree that Roosevelt was involved in the attack on Pearl Harbor, they are not all that radical. For example, although the historians Charles Callan Tansill (1890-1964) and Charles Austin Beard (1874-1948) criticised him for leading his country into the war on account of his foreign policy, they refuted the claim that the president intentionally caused the Japanese offensive in Pearl Harbor.

It is necessary to put the theories accusing Roosevelt of complicity into perspective for a number of reasons:

- First of all, the messages from Japan were often mysterious and difficult to decipher.
- Next, if the president deliberately concealed what he knew about Japan's intentions, many people would have been linked to the plot, such as his subordinates and everybody who saw the telegram. Consequently, it is entirely plausible to imagine that the secret would have come out.
- Finally, to this day no document or other source has been found to support the theory that Roosevelt wanted the attack on the American fleet at Pearl Harbor.

In any case, the attack on the naval base remains one of the most important events in the history of the United States. Over 75 years later, the Japanese raid against the American fleet continues to stir up strong feelings and still the object of numerous studies today.

SUMMARY

1941

26th July: Oil and steel embargo and freezing of Japanese assets on US soil

6th Sept.: Japan decides to go to war unless an agreement is reached

3rd Nov.: Plan to attack Pearl Harbor approved

7th Dec.: Surprise attack on Pearl Harbor

8th Dec.: Japan declares war on the USA and Great Britain

10th Dec.: USA enters the war

- Since the 1930s, Japan and the United States had been competing for dominance over the territories and trade in the Pacific. Discussions between the two major powers quickly deteriorated and, faced with deadlock, in September 1941 Japan decided to go to war against its adversary.
- On 7 December, Japan launched its offensive against the American air and naval base at Pearl Harbor.
- Led by Isoroku Yamamoto, the attack unfolded in two successive phases. In two hours, the American naval

fleet was destroyed and a large number of planes were damaged.

- Losses were high, especially for the Americans, of whom over 2000 died and around 1000 were wounded.
- Although the attack ended in success for the Japanese, their victory was not total. The American repair shops and fuel depots were spared by the Japanese bombs and gunfire, which allowed the Americans to recover.
- Furthermore, the attack had serious consequences, because it marked the United States' entry into the war: now, the conflict was global.
- Immediately after the attack, the United States authorities tried to establish who was to blame for the raid and its outcome. The admiral Husband Edward Kimmel and the general Walter Campbell Short were quickly accused of negligence and stripped of their functions.

We want to hear from you!
Leave a comment on your online library
and share your favourite books on social media!

FIND OUT MORE

BIBLIOGRAPHY

- Arroyo, E. (2003) *Pearl Harbor*. New York: MetroBooks.
- Chan, M. (2016) 'A Date Which Will Live in Infamy.' Read President Roosevelt's Pearl Harbor Address. *Time*. [Online]. [Accessed 24 January 2017]. Available from: <http://time.com/4593483/pearl-harbor-franklin-roosevelt-infamy-speech-attack/>
- Costello, J. (1982) *The Pacific War*. New York: William Morrow.
- Delmas, C. (2001) *Pearl Harbor. La guerre devient mondiale*. Paris: Éditions Complexe.
- Garrity, J.A. (1974) *Dictionnaire biographique américain*. New York: Charles Scribners' Sons.
- Hixson, W. (2003) *The American Experience in World War II*, volume 4. New York: Routledge.
- Hugues, A.T. (2009) Yamamoto Isoroku. *Encyclopedia Britannica*. [Online]. [Accessed 24 January 2017]. Available from: <https://www.britannica.com/biography/Yamamoto-Isoroku>
- Kaspi, A. (1987) Pearl Harbor, une provocation américaine ? *L'Histoire*, issue 101, pp. 36-44.
- Kaspi, A. (1997) *Franklin Roosevelt*. Paris: Fayard.
- Kimmel, H.E. (1955) *Admiral Kimmel's Story*. Chicago: Henry Regnery Company.
- Lord, W. (1999) *Day of Infamy: Attack on Pearl Harbor*. Ware, Hertfordshire: Wordsworth Editions Limited.
- Médiathèque (no date) *Attaque sur Pearl Harbor*. [Online]. [Accessed 14 January 2014]. Available

from: <http://www.mediatheque-fm6.ma/index2.
php?option=com_docman&task=doc_view&gid=796&I-
temid=78>
- Michel, H. (1975) *Second World War*. London:
  HarperCollins.
- Mourre, M. (no date) Pearl Harbor. *Dictionnaire encyclo-
  pédique d'histoire*. Paris: Bordas.
- Naval History and Heritage Command (no date) *Pearl
  Harbor Raid*. [Online]. [Accessed 24 January 2017].
  Available from: <https://www.history.navy.mil/our-col-
  lections/photography/wars-and-events/world-war-ii/
  pearl-harbor-raid.html>
- Prange, G.W. (1991) *At Dawn We Slept: The Untold Story
  of Pearl Harbor*. London: Penguin.
- *Seconds from Disaster: Pearl Harbor*. (2011)
  [Documentary]. Sean Smith. Dir. USA.
- Smith, C. (2004) *Pearl Harbor 1941: The Day of Infamy*.
  London: Praeger.
- Theobald, R.A. (2006) *The Final Secret of Pearl Harbor*.
  Pomeroy, Washington: Health Service Books.
- Toland, J. (1982) *Infamy: Pearl Harbor and its Aftermath*.
  New York: Doubleday.
- Wohlstetter, R. (1962) *Pearl Harbor: Warning and
  Decision*. California: Stanford University Press.

ADDITIONAL SOURCES

- Asada, S. (2006) *From Mahan to Pearl Harbor: The
  Imperial Japanese Navy and the United States*. Annapolis:
  Naval Institute Press.
- Cohen, S. (2001) *Attack on Pearl Harbor: A Pictorial*

History. Missoula, Montana: Pictorial Histories
  Publishing Co.
* Ienaga, S. (1978) *The Pacific War 1931-1945*. New York:
  Pantheon Books.
* Iriye, A. (1981) *Power and Culture: The Japanese-American
  War, 1941-1945*. Cambridge, Massachusetts: Harvard
  University Press.
* Nelson, C. (2016) *Pearl Harbor: From Infamy to Greatness*.
  London: Weidenfeld & Nicolson.
* Turtledove, H. (2005) *Days of Infamy*. New York: New
  American Library.
* Victor, G. (2006) *The Pearl Harbor Myth: Rethinking the
  Unthinkable*. Washington: Potomac Books.
* Willmott, H.P. (2001) *Pearl Harbor*. London: Orion
  Publishing.

ICONOGRAPHIC SOURCES

* Photograph taken during the signing of the Treaty of
  Versailles. Royalty-free reproduction picture.
* Portrait of General Walter Campbell Short. Royalty-free
  reproduction picture.
* Photograph of Admiral Yamamoto, taken in 1940.
  Royalty-free reproduction picture.
* Aerial view of the Pearl Harbor military base shortly
  before the Japanese attack. Royalty-free reproduction
  picture.
* Detailed preparation for the attack on a model. © US
  Navy National Museum of Naval Aviation.
* Japanese planes ready for takeoff to attack Pearl Harbor.
  © Henry Sakaida.

FILMS

- *From Here to Eternity.* (1953) [Film]. Fred Zinneman. Dir. USA: Columbia Pictures Corporation.
- *Tora! Tora! Tora!* (1970) [Film]. Richard Fleischer. Dir. USA/Japan: Twentieth Century-Fox.
- *1941.* (1979) [Film]. Steven Spielberg. Dir. USA: Universal Pictures, Columbia Pictures Corporation, A-Team.
- *The Final Countdown.* (1980) [Film]. Don Taylor. Dir. USA: The Bryna Company.
- *Pearl Harbor.* (2001) [Film]. Michael Bay. Dir. USA: Touchstone Pictures.

MUSEUMS AND COMMEMORATIVE BUILDINGS

- Pacific Aviation Museum Pearl Harbor, Honolulu, Ohau.
- USS Arizona Memorial, Pearl Harbor, Hawaii.

www.50minutes.com

Ebook EAN: 9782806289735

Paperback EAN: 9782806293770

Legal Deposit: D/2017/12603/69

Cover: © Primento

Digital conception by Primento, the digital partner of publishers.